MY NAME IS SCHNUCKIPUTZ

JUST CALL ME SCHNUCKI

An interactive children's story designed to encourage positive conversations between a child and parent or caregiver

Rosemarie Ingrid Dinklage, Author

Inge Cibis, Illustrator

CONTENTS

ACKNOWLEDGMENTS

I started writing about Schnucki a long time ago. My friend Alice Primack encouraged me, over the years, to write a children's book about Schnucki's life and adventures. Alice never let me give up but kept pushing me to continue. Other friends helped with editing or just encouraging me. These are Dr. Maria Alvarez, Dr. Stephen and Michele Borst, Janet Davies, Dr. Kathy Funke, Dr. Carolyn Lawrence, Ruth Raymer, Janice Russell, Sharon Watts, and Elizabeth Zorilo.

Selina Gould read some of the stories to her 6-year-old son Neriah. He enjoyed listening to the stories and asked and responded to questions. Marshall Bloom, a retired technical writer and editor, just knew what needed fixing - from plain word choice and punctuation to the overall organization. I am grateful to Chris Monahan, who went over the agreement between Everfield Press and me; his help was invaluable to me. My friend Inge Cibis came all the way from Germany to illustrate this book. Thank you, Inge.

Last but not least, I would like to thank Karen Porter, the owner of Everfield Press, for her time, patience and guidance (choosing the color, size, font, format, and many other decisions) to help me put these stories into a book.

FOREWORD

This book is an interactive children's story designed to encourage positive conversations between the child and a parent or caregiver. Dr. Dinklage is focusing on feelings from sadness to absolute joy! Schnucki died unexpectedly, which left Dr. Dinklage with feelings of utter sadness. Her fond memories helped her process her emotions. She hopes they will help parents and children process emotions too. These true stories are for all who want to build their emotional intelligence. Parents and caregivers are encouraged to read stories to the child that fit what is happening in the child's life now.

My Name is Schnuckiputz

DEDICATION

To Schnucki and her four-legged friends

MY FRIENDS AND FAMILY

Name	Color	Picture
Eeny	Orange	
Meeny	Grey	
Miny	Calico	
Moe	Black and White	
Princess Ma Cherie	Black	
SuzieQ	Black and White	
Enrico	Tan, Brown and White	

My Name is Schnuckiputz

My Name is Schnuckiputz

1

HI I'M SCHNUCKI

I am a long-haired Chihuahua. My ancestors came from Mexico. My Mom calls me Schnuckiputz. That is a German word that means "little darling" or "sweetheart." She also calls me Schnucki or Young Lady. All I do is walk down the street and Mom calls "Young Laaaaaady!"

When I am good, she calls me Schnuckiputz-I-Love-You or Schnuckiputz-I-Love-You-Immerzu, which is German for Schnuckiputz-I-Love-You-All-The-Time.

My middle name is Spoiled Rotten - Mom says that doesn't need an explanation.

One time, Mom and I went to the bank. All the cashiers wanted to see me (because I am so cute), so I just walked along the counter. When Mom called "Schnuckiputz come back," a young man turned around and he explained that his mother called him Schnuckiputz when he was a child. He had never heard the name Schnuckiputz outside of his home.

Robert, a friend of the family, calls me Schnuckum. He never calls me by any other name - even when I peed on his bathroom rug. Oops!

Q

Do your friends call you nice things, even when you have peed on their rug?

2

MEET SCHNUCKI'S FAMILY

I live with my Mom, my adopted sister SusieQ and five cats. They go by the names of Eeny, Meeny, Miny, Moe, and Princess Ma Cherie.

My Name is Schnuckiputz

3

MAKING DECISIONS - SCHNUCKI'S BIRTHDAY PARTY

When I turned four, my Mom decided that I could have a birthday party. She asked me whom I wanted to invite. First, she gave me rules. I could only invite friends that do not bark, fight, or are mean. They could not poop or pee in the house or be a real nuisance.

My Mom invited about 15 people and I could invite three friends. I invited my sister SusieQ and two friends who met my Mom's rules.

My Mom and her friends had pizza and fancy drinks.. Two friends came with Schatzi, a Pekingese. My Mom's friend Brenda came with Madeleine, a greyhound, whose birthday was a week later. Brenda made a real nice birthday cake for us. She used canned dog food, tuna, and some other yummy stuff. She also brought four candles and plates that said, "Happy Birthday." Everybody brought us a card and gifts. My favorite card was sent by a friend of my Mom's who lives in South Florida. It read "The Princess Turned 4." Madeleine and I got matching sweaters as presents. The guests had so much fun that they kept asking my Mom to give another party.

Q

Do you have birthday parties?
Whom do you invite? Are there any rules?

4

SCHNUCKI'S LIKES,
DISLIKES, AND FEARS

LIKES:

Food

- Steak
- Tuna
- Salad with a nice dressing
- Apples
- Salami

Activities

- Sleeping
- Listening to music
- Playing with other dogs
- Going to church
- Taking treats away from my sister
- Going to TGIF (Thank God It's Friday) parties with my Mom
- Riding in the car
- Sitting on my Mom's lap
- Sitting in the sun
- Visiting with friends
- Traveling with my Mom
- Being the center of attention

Q What do you like?

DISLIKES:

- Going to the vet
- Going out in the rain
- Sharing treats with my sister
- Eating dry dog food
- Mom going out or traveling without me

Q   What do you dislike?

FEARS:

- Getting shots at the vet
- Getting stuck in the sand on the beach
- Traveling on the plane when I can't sit on my Mom's lap
- Not understanding people in foreign countries
- Busses coming too close to the curb when I am walking on the sidewalk

- Going into an elevator or on an escalator
- Street noise from cars, taxis, busses, streetcars, and sirens
- Falling into the swimming pool

Q

What are some of your fears?
Can you talk to someone about them?

My Name is Schnuckiputz

5

BEING BRAVE WHEN FACING
A SCARY EXPERIENCE

Schnucki's First Airplane Ride

My Name is Schnuckiputz

My Mom told me we were going to visit
relatives in Kansas City. We would be taking
an airplane. I had never been on an airplane.
A friend of my Mom's took us to the airport.
Mom made sure that I peed on the grass next
to the terminal before we checked our
luggage and went through the security check.
After that my Mom had to put me in a carrier
to take me on the plane. The flight attendant
told Mom that she would have to put the
carrier underneath her seat for take-off. I
didn't like that a bit!

I was scared stiff. The engines were so loud.
I did not know what was happening. The
flight attendant told Mom that I could sit on
her lap once we were up in the air and at
cruising altitude. I was shaking but I did not
whine or cry. Mom did not waste a second
getting me out of the carrier and putting me
on her lap. Then it was fun. Mom showed
me the clouds. It was like riding in a car. I

love car rides because I get to sit on my Mom's lap, and I can see the clouds through the moon-roof.

On the flight back, the flight attendant told my Mom that I was well behaved and seemed to be a seasoned traveler. When Mom called me "Schnuckiputz-I-Love-You," I knew she was proud of me.

Q

Have you ever been scared? What happened?

6

LEARNING TO TRUST - FALLING INTO THE POOL

When my Mom bought a new house, it did not have a swimming pool. So, my Mom had one put in, making sure the steps would not be too deep so I could get out, in case I might fall in. Not too long after the completion of the pool, my Mom was standing by the pool, with me in her arms. She twisted her foot and, before we knew it, we were in the water. My Mom said she was not worried about me because she knew I could swim. Well, I was so scared that I did not get near the pool unless my Mom was around. For some reason, I thought my Mom made us fall into the pool on purpose.

I did fall in one night. My Mom was sitting in the living room and the door was open. She heard a sound and thought that the pool pump had turned on, which was strange because it was 10 o'clock at night. I did a lot of splashing to get her attention. I was in the deep end of the pool and far away from the steps. I was so scared. When my Mom came out of the house, she told me to swim to her which I did. She then fished me out. I was so happy that I licked her face. I just love my Mom.

Q

Do you remember a time when you were scared? Do you remember how happy you were when you saw your mom or your dad?

7

EMPATHY –
SCHNUCKI'S FIRST ADVENTURE IN HER
NEW HOME

When I first came to live with my Mom, she was sad because her dog had died. I wanted to make her laugh, so I tried many things. First, I chased butterflies around the yard.

I could not catch one because I could not jump high enough. They just flew away laughing at me. That made my Mom laugh too!

Then I saw a bull on the other side of the
fence. I chased the bull which was fun. I
figured my Mom would just love it. Love
what? Well, of course, my chasing the bull.
But, all of a sudden, the bull turned around!
I stared into his eyes. He did not like the
confrontation and he still tried to chase me!
My Mom saw everything. She was so worried
she called me to come home. I went home
because I did not want my Mom to be upset.

Q

How about you? How do you feel when your parents are worried and get upset?
What kinds of things do you do to make them laugh?

My Name is Schnuckiputz

8

COPING WITH SAD FEELINGS - GOING TO ENRICO

Sometimes I just get sad. I bet all Chihuahuas do, from time to time. My Mom bought this big doll in Mexico City (there are lots of Chihuahuas in Mexico!) and I love him. We named him Enrico.

Whenever I am sad, I just go and cuddle up with Enrico. It really helps.

Q

Where do you go when you are sad? Does it help?

My Name is Schnuckiputz

9

MEMORIES OF FRIENDS

You might remember that my friend Madeleine came to my birthday party. Everybody liked her because she was sweet and not selfish.

One time when we were vacationing a big thunderstorm came up.

Of course, Madeleine and I can hear these
things before our Moms can. Madeleine ran
to the bathroom and curled herself around
the toilet. She was very, very scared and she
shivered all over her body. I was scared too.
But knowing how Madeleine felt, I sat next to
her and talked to her, trying to calm her
down.

Although Madeleine is a greyhound, she was never in dog races. When she came to visit us, she would run all over the yard as fast as lightening. I was not able to do that. Madeleine said that this was okay. She was always understanding.

The last time Madeleine came to visit us she did not seem to be feeling well. Her mom told us that Madeleine had cancer. I didn't know what that meant. I thought she had a cold or something and would be well soon. When I asked Madeleine about it, she looked really sad, but didn't want to talk about it. Sometimes I think that she did not know what the word "cancer" meant either. She probably had some idea that it was not something good. A short time after Madeleine's visit my Mom told me that Madeleine had died and that she had gone to dog heaven.

When my Mom and I were in Europe, a friend looked after SusieQ and Eeny, Meeny, Miny, Moe, and Princess Ma Cherie. Meeny got sick and had to be taken to the vet. After examining Meeny, the vet told our friend that Meeny has to be put to sleep; she was going to die. When we came back and heard the news, my Mom cried a lot. I miss Madeleine the most. Sometimes I get sad, but then I try to think of all the fun we had together. That helps a lot.

Q

Did you ever have to bury a dog or a cat, or some other animal who had become your friend? How did you feel when that happened?

My Name is Schnuckiputz

10

BEING AFRAID -
A VISIT TO THE VET

Vet is short for veterinarian and means
animal doctor. When SusieQ and I have to go

to the vet, we love the attention and the treats. The last time we went, SusieQ was shaking the moment we were shown into the examining room. My Mom told us that we needed to have our nails trimmed. Well, when we got there, they told my Mom that our shots were due. That made SusieQ very upset; she was ready to go home - and so was I. They also had to take our blood. My Mom told the vet that she understood why we were nervous because she gets very nervous when her doctors take her blood.

They told my Mom that I got a shot for some virus and that SusieQ did not get one. My Mom had no idea how this happened. I was happy that I did not have to have another shot, but I felt sorry for SusieQ. Mom told the vet that one of her friends (just one?) claimed that she prefers me over SusieQ, but she would never go as far as having different medical treatments for us. I think she gives SusieQ a larger piece of steak or cheese. Trust me, I can tell the difference in sizes. Her halves are always larger than mine.

The vet told Mom that we need to come back in a year. Boy, we were ready to get out of there and go home - so was Mom. When we were in the car, Mom explained to us that the shots are very important to keep both of us healthy.

Q

How do you feel when you have to see a doctor or dentist? Do you get nervous? Do they talk to you or only to your parents?

My Name is Schnuckiputz

11

FACING CHALLENGES - TRYING NEW THINGS GOING TO THE BEACH

The first time I went to the beach, I wanted to go right back home. I was scared stiff of the waves with their loud crashing sound and spray. Also, I didn't like sinking into the sand or getting my feet wet. Ugg!

But I saw other dogs and people splashing in the water and playing in the sand, and I wanted to have fun too. So, I tried it again. And again.

Now I go to the beach all the time and I love
it! I don't even mind the sand and the wet
feet. It's all part of the fun. The birds love it
when I run after them and I do too.

Q

Is there anything that you didn't like at first
and now you think it's fun?
What do you think happened?

My Name is Schnuckiputz

My Name is Schnuckiputz

12

JEALOUSY-
SCHNUCKI GETS A SISTER

My Mom decided that I should have a sister
so that I am not alone when she is not at
home. She said, "Let's go to Pet Rescue to
find a sister." We went. Mom liked SusieQ.
She was a mix of a short-hair Chihuahua and
a Jack Russel. She seemed to be sweet and
full of vigor. But I thought that she was ugly

55

(she had this underbite) and her eyes were funny (each one looked in a different direction). My Mom said, "Her middle name is Ms. Ugly." We took her home. I had trouble with her the first few days because she always had these teeth sticking out and she never seemed to look at me. But my other siblings (5 cats: Eeny, Meeny, Miny, Moe, and Princess Ma Cherie) liked her. They did not make any fuss when she came to live with us.

When you hear Ma Cherie, you are probably thinking of these chocolates called Mon Cheries. A friend of my Mom's just loves them. My Mom buys them for her when she goes to Germany. But Ma Cherie means my darling and has nothing to do with chocolates.

I was worried my Mom would prefer SusieQ and give her all the attention. She would give her more food and treats and play with her and not with me. I also thought that my friends and my Mom's friends would like her better.

Q

Would you be worried if you were to get a sister or brother?
What would you be worried about?

My Name is Schnuckiputz

My Name is Schnuckiputz

13

BEING HELPFUL -
MY SISTER SUSIEQ

I helped my Mom with SusieQ. When we
were not watching her, she would leave the

yard and run into the street. Whenever she did this, I would bark really loud so my Mom would know she was doing it again. SusieQ scared me because she would not look out for cars or the mail carrier when he stopped at the mailbox.

Q

Do you help your mom and dad? If so, how?

When we first got SusieQ, my Mom took us to a party. It was a party for children. SusieQ almost freaked out! She did not like little children. She snapped at them. My Mom was a school psychologist and knows a lot about children. She told me that SusieQ had been abused, most likely by young children, and that is why she reacts this way. SusieQ even nipped a neighbor's daughter and had to be quarantined. She had to stay home for a long time and could not come with us. My

Mom made sure that SusieQ did not get close to young children. She was ok with older children and grown-ups.

Q

Do you have a brother or sister (or an animal) you have to watch out for?
Can you help your parents and how do you do it?

My Name is Schnuckiputz

14

BEING SNEAKY -
SCNUCKI LOVES TO TAKE HER SISTER'S
TREATS AWAY

One day, my Mom put one treat in front of
me and one in front of my sister SusieQ. I

took mine and put it in a safe place far enough from her. Then I decided I wanted hers as well. So, I stood in front of her and looked at her to make sure she saw me. I then turned my head and barked, telling her I saw something in the corner. Of course, SusieQ looked in that direction to see what was happening. This gave me time to take her treat and walk off with it.

That was sneaky!

Q Would you do something like that?

Well, I can tell you another story. My friend Schatzi, a Pekingese, came to visit us for a weekend. My Mom had to go out for a few hours and left us at home. Schatzi and I took a nap - that's what I thought. Guess what, the next day my Mom happened to talk to a neighbor. He said, "Schatzi was walking around the neighborhood for about an hour or a little longer."

Well, Mom found out that he went through the doggy door in the house and got into the yard. Nothing unusual because that's where we go when we pee and poop. The person who cut the grass left the gate open. Guess what? Schatzi sneaked out and walked all over the neighborhood! When he was done, he came back through the open gate and then through the pet door. If Mom had not talked to the neighbor, we would not have known he had sneaked out.

Q   What do you think about that?

My Name is Schnuckiputz

My Name is Schnuckiputz

15

SCHNUCKI'S SIBLINGS - EENY, MEENY, MINY, MOE AND PRINCESS MA CHERIE

Let me tell you all about my siblings Eeny, Meeny, Miny, Moe, and Princess Ma Cherie. When my Mom bought her house from a friend, she heard that two cats, Eeny and

Moe, came with it. They were about 6 months old and loved to play. Although Eeny was friendly, he did not play much with his siblings Meeny, Miny, Moe, and Princess Ma Cherie.

Mr. Moe took very long walks. He said "hello" to the horses next to my Mom's property. He walked along the side of the street. My Mom thought he visited his girlfriend.

One day she came to visit. Mr. Moe and she screamed at each other. It seemed to go on for hours. We didn't know what was going on. When Mom drove up in her Mercedes,

Mr. Moe knew the sound of the engine. He made sure there was no car around. Then he crossed the street.

Once, my Mom and an aunt visited a friend who had found a cat. The friend wanted my Mom to take the cat home. She had four cats and they all looked just like Meeny. They all had grey fur. We named her "Meeny Wunschkind." My Mom said that Meeny sounded like a mean cat and so she added the German word "Wunschkind," which means a child that is wished for. On the way home, she sat on the aunt's lap and looked out the window. Meeny wanted to make sure she knew where we were going. At home, she was always curious. When a handyman came, she sat on top of the door and watched, if necessary, all day.

We had a telephone on the wall next to a bar
stool. Meeny would jump onto the chair and
hit my Mom with her paws again and again
on both sides of her face until my Mom left
to use another phone.

My sibling Miny is another story. My Mom
found her in our yard on Thanksgiving Day.
She was a calico cat and about six months
old. Calico cats have fur of different colors
and are usually girls. Miny liked to sit on the
steps leading into the house. She had eyes
that looked like a slit, and she inspected
everyone who wanted to enter the house.
Miny always knew what she wanted and
knew how to get it. She would look at the
door leading outdoors and then at my Mom.
She did this until my Mom opened the door

for her. Miny also did this when she wanted extra food. She looked at the container holding the food and then at my Mom. When Mom didn't give her anything, she would stamp her foot and scream "Mom!" My Mom let her do this a few times, because she thought that it was funny and unusual for a cat to behave this way. Miny loved it when my Mom sang an aria from the opera "Aida." Mom usually only sings when she is taking a shower. Mom would sing "Miny" instead of "Aida." Miny would purr and swish her tail like she was conducting the opera.

My Mom and I cannot remember how Princess Ma Cherie came to live with us. We just remember that she was tiny and always the smallest of the five cats. We also remember that when we named her Princess Ma Cherie a friend of my Mom said, "that's an awfully long name for a tiny cat like her." I remember one time when my Mom found a tick on her and she got sick. She was gasping for air. The vet told my Mom that she might die. Mom was so upset. For what seemed like a whole year, my Mom got up every night to give her medicine. She mixed some drops with canned tuna. That helped right away.

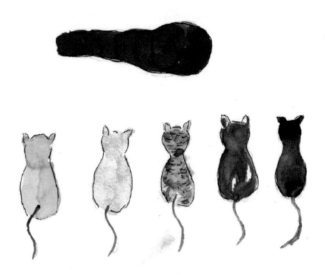

I have another funny story to tell you. My Mom went grocery shopping and bought herself an expensive lobster tail. Since she did not know whether Eeny, Meeny, Miny, Moe, and Princess Ma Cherie liked lobster, she gave each one a taste. All five of them jumped about 3 feet high and begged for more. Well, my Mom decided right then and there that she would never bring lobster tail home again!

Now you know the stories about Eeny, Meeny, Miny, Moe, and Princess Ma Cherie.

Q

Which of the cats is your favorite? Would you take him or her home?

My Name is Schnuckiputz

16

GETTING LOST-
DAYTONA BEACH AND THE KENNEDY
SPACE CENTER

When my Mom's niece Didi came to visit, all
of us went to Daytona Beach. Robert, a friend
of the family, joined us to go to the Kennedy
Space Center.

They left in the morning except for SusieQ
and me. I tried to tell my Mom that SusieQ
had sneaked out of the hotel room, but they
were so busy getting ready that nobody

listened to me. I was worried about SusieQ
because she is so nosy and sometimes she
just does not think or look right or left to see
whether cars are coming. When they came
back, which was much later than they had
hoped, they could not find SusieQ. My Mom
went to the office of the hotel, but nobody
knew anything.

My Mom went to the office again the next
morning, and she was told that the people
working in the office found SusieQ in the
parking lot. They kept her all day and then
called the police who picked her up. I may
have told you that SusieQ is nice and polite.
She was so scared that they didn't want her
to go to Pet Rescue. They all took turns
looking after SusieQ. They even asked the
Gainesville Police Department to send a

policeman to our neighborhood to find out if they knew where my Mom is.

My Mom met somebody from the Daytona Beach Police Department to get SusieQ. My Mom wanted to give the lady some money to go out to lunch because they took so much trouble looking after SusieQ. But she would not take it.

When we got home, I sent a nice letter to the Daytona Beach Police Department thanking them for all the trouble. My Mom could not give me a street address, but I was sure that the post office could find the police department. Well, the letter came back! Can you believe this? My Mom then mailed the letter to her friend Robert, who took it to the police department.

Q What would you do if your brother or sister or your pet got lost?

My Name is Schnuckiputz

My Name is Schnuckiputz

17

SCHNUCKI'S TRIP TO CHARLESTON, NORTH CAROLINA

The first time my Mom took me to
Charleston, we were getting out of the car

when a man called, "You can't take this dog out of the car. She needs to wear a muzzle." I must have scared him. But I would never bite anybody. Then we went into a furniture store. My Mom was carrying me. The moment we entered the store, someone said, "Here comes a second opinion." When my Mom went for a walk and was carrying me, people asked, "Is this what you call walking your dog?" They all had such a good sense of humor.

In St. Augustine everything changed. We could only walk a few steps before someone would want to know what kind of dog I am, how old I am, what my name is etc. Now that we have SusieQ as well, we never get very far. I want to tell you about my second trip to Charleston. That time, Brenda and SusieQ came along. Actually, Brenda was driving because she knew the way and she loves to drive. I don't think I have to tell you about the restaurant scene, because in America most places don't let pets into the restaurant. My Mom and Brenda went to dinner, but SusieQ and I had to stay in the hotel. My Mom always takes our beds along. So, when we stayed at the hotel, she put my bed on hers so that I could get comfortable. Brenda did the same for SusieQ. But the moment Brenda put SusieQ into bed, she bit Brenda right on the lips and chin. We were stunned because she had never done that before, but Brenda got right into her face and that scared SusieQ. Brenda was still nice to SusieQ the next day. But now nobody in my family trusts her.

The next morning, we all went to a plantation. Again, SusieQ and I had to stay in the car. My Mom told me that the gardens were absolutely beautiful. They had lots of azaleas that were in bloom. These gardens were built by 100 slaves, and it took them 10 years! Charleston had too much traffic for my taste and too many people. Sometimes I really don't mind staying in the car because the we can sleep and do not have to face the crowds. And I don't have to walk.

Q

Can you think of any trips you have taken that you enjoyed and have fond memories of?

My Name is Schnuckiputz

My Name is Schnuckiputz

18

SCHNUCKI'S TRIP TO KANSAS CITY, KANSAS

Mom told me that our relatives have a dog called Touchdown and that he was a lab (short for Labrador). Sometimes my Mom says that I am a lap dog. I thought she meant that Touchdown was a lap dog too. He was a huge caring and loving dog. He protected their daughter, Cathy. I promise you would not have gone near Cathy when Touchdown was around. I think he would have made chopped meat out of you.

Mom and a friend went out to lunch and did some shopping. I kept Touchdown company. After some time, I started worrying about my Mom. Because Touchdown and I were in the backyard, I decided to explore it. I found this hole big enough for me to get out. Touchdown was upset, but I could not worry about him and my Mom. I had to go and find her. I walked out of the yard and down the street. I didn't know where I was or where to find my Mom, so I turned around. When I got back to the house, there was a couple across the street with three dogs.

Mom told me to always be friendly and polite, so I walked across the street and said "hello." When they realized I was looking for my Mom, they called the number on my collar which was our phone number in Florida. They called five times. They were on their way to the park. They felt that they could not take me along, so they put me in the back yard. My Mom told me later that she was upset when she could not find me. She said, "Maybe somebody called my home, but I cannot remember all these pin numbers." My Mom asked a lady who was driving by whether she had seen me. She said, "a neighbor found a little white dog," and she knew where I was. When my Mom found me, both my Mom and I were ecstatic. What a happy ending!

What did my Mom and I learn?

Also big dogs are loving and caring.

My Mom will know how to access her answering machine. I will not run off, and I will trust my Mom to come back.

Q

How about you?

Have you had a scary experience?

How did you feel?

What did you learn?

My Name is Schnuckiputz

My Name is Schnuckiputz

19

SCHNUCKI'S TRIP TO KEY WEST, FLORIDA

I, my sister SusieQ, my Mom and her niece
Didi went to Key Largo where we met Robert,
a friend of the family. Didi went with Robert
on his Harley motorcycle from there. Mom
and I followed them in the car. It was a long
trip because there was so much traffic.
The Bed and Breakfast we stayed at was nice
and had a swimming pool. SusieQ and I
don't like to swim, but all the others do. We
went out to dinner to celebrate Robert's
birthday, but we could not go into the dining
room. The Health Department does not
permit this. I think this is strange because
my Mom took me to restaurants in Europe. I
could go to any restaurant.

The next day, we all went to the Hemingway
House. Robert and Didi went inside. The rest
of us stayed outside. The man who collects
the tickets told my Mom that we should not
be on the property because SusieQ and I

would scare the cats. A few of the 61 cats came up and stared at us. They all had six toes. I had never seen six-toed cats before. I think they had never seen dogs before.

Then we went to the lighthouse. My Mom's right knee hurts when she climbs

stairs. Didi was the only one who went all
the way up. Some kids said that there were
85 steps. Didi did not offer to take me - I
could have made it up! All she had to do was
carry me down because I am afraid going
down steps. After that, we did an awful lot
of walking. I don't like to walk, but SusieQ
does. She could walk all day.

In the evening, we went to Mallory Square.
Everybody was waiting for the sun to set.
People go there a couple of hours early to see
street performers. Some swallow fire, others
have animals perform tricks, and some dance
and sing. A lot of people came over to talk
to SusieQ and me. That part we liked, but
not being among so many people.

The next morning, we all went to the beach.
I didn't like the beach - neither did my Mom.
There were too many stones and no sand. I
liked it better when we went to see Robert in
Daytona Beach. His apartment is right on the
beach and the beach is beautiful. It is very

wide, has fine sand, and there are no cars allowed on the beach in front of his building. We all went to town. Didi drove - she learned how to drive in Germany where she lives. She told me that driving here is boring. In Germany, she goes 240 km an hour (that's about 160 miles) on the Autobahn. The Autobahn is a highway and generally does not have a speed limit. I rode with Didi. That is fast. I was happy - NO walking. My Mom is nice, she carries me a lot. That way, I can also see lots of things - not just legs.

Q Have you been to Key West or would you like to go?

My Name is Schnuckiputz

20

SCHNUCKI GOES TO EUROPE

I said goodbye to Eeny, Meeny, Miny, Moe, and Princess Ma Cherie as well as to SusieQ and my friend Enrico.

The trip to Europe was a lot of fun once we were there. Being on an airplane for 10 hours straight is not much fun. My Mom asked the flight attendant why she had to pay for my flight. The flight attendant claimed it was because of the service. My Mom told her that I would like champagne and filet mignon (for those of you who do not know French yet, filet mignon means steak - but a really expensive one). They didn't give me anything, not even some water!

I went with my Mom wherever she went. When we got to the mall, my Mom had to carry me on the escalator. When we went to a restaurant, they offered a bench seat so that I could sit next to my Mom. Can you imagine that? Well, I didn't.

My Mom's sister had a hunting dog, but he was afraid of me. Or was he a very nice host? He had a bed that I would take a nap in. My Mom's sister was furious with me. Then I jumped on the sofa and sat on a cushion.

She practically fainted. When I moved to the
love seat that was supposed to be for her
dog, she almost threw us out. My Mom told
her, "All you are telling Schnucki is the
places she cannot sit in. How about telling
her where she **can** sit?" Then her sister
wanted to know why I can't sit under the
table like other dogs. You see, when you go
to a restaurant in Europe - even those with 5
stars (that means they are very, very

expensive) - all dogs sit under the table. My
Mom told her that in America you can't take
a dog to a restaurant unless it's outdoors,
and even then, most don't allow it. I had
never learned to sit under a table.

We went to Germany in July. It was cold and
it rained a lot. My Mom told me that once it
rains it gets cold. She always put me under
her raincoat, but I still shivered a lot. I was

cold even though I have a fur coat. My Mom
was so cold she had to buy some warm
clothes, the kind she wears during the winter
in Florida.

Then we took the train to Switzerland. My
Mom met one of her German friends in
Zurich, a large, beautiful city. My Mom and I
went out to dinner the first night. She asked
the waiter if I could sit on a chair next to her.
He was not sure. So, my Mom put me on the
floor. Just then a native came by. My Mom
explained that a native is someone who lives
in Zurich. He said to me, "The floor is much
too cold and hard for you. Why don't you
come and sit on my lap?" I just loved him.
He told us that he has a German Shepherd at
home.
The next day, we went to a park and a cafe. A
cafe is a fancy coffee shop that has fabulous
pastries. It was right next to the street so you

could watch the people go by. They do that a lot in Europe.

Q

Do you have pleasant memories of a trip?

What are they?

Have you ever visited another state or another country?

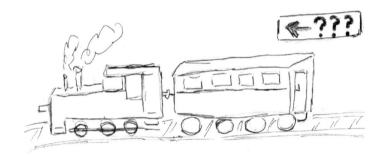

THE END

My Name is Schnuckiputz

ABOUT THE AUTHOR

Dr. Rosemarie Dinklage was born in Reppen, a city east of Berlin in Germany. When Rosemarie was 6 years old, she and her family - her mother and three sibling ages 1 1/2, 4 and 15 - fled when the Russian soldiers invaded Germany. The family left on the very last train and settled in the Harz mountains.

When Dr. Dinklage was 15, the family moved to Mannheim, south of Frankfurt. At age 21, she spent 6 months as an au-pair in northern England. Less than a year later she was offered and accepted a position as a bilingual secretary in New York City. Years later, she worked as a translator and received her B.A. degree from Hunter College. She obtained her M.A. degree in school psychology at the University of South Florida and then worked for several years. Upon her husband's death in 1980, she moved to Gainesville and earned her Ph.D. at the University of Florida. Her dissertation topic was

Children's Perception of War and Peace and the subjects were American and German 4th graders.

Dr. Dinklage retired from her career as a school psychologist and is now living with her dog Cloe, her seventh rescue dog. She enjoys reading, going to the theatre, meeting friends for dinner, and traveling whenever possible. She also enjoys writing about her adopted four-legged children. She has fond memories of her five cats and six dogs. All taught her valuable lessons.

ABOUT THE ILLUSTRATOR

Inge Cibis is an artist from Germany who works primarily with watercolors. Inge learned to paint as therapy for arthritis pain when she was 30. She started taking classes to learn to paint to release her pain. She has since exhibited her work at local art festivals in Germany, where she lives. Inge has three grown children.

Made in the USA
Columbia, SC
17 January 2020